Skunks

Written by Adrienne Mason

Illustrated by Nancy Gray Ogle

KIDS CAN PRESS

WILDLIFE SERIES

Kids Can Press

For Noella, who appreciates nature, smells and all — AM

For Audrey Tournay — NGO

I would like to thank Professor Jerry Dragoo of the Museum of Southwestern Biology,
University of New Mexico, for his manuscript review and consultation.

Text © 2006 Adrienne Mason
Illustrations © 2006 Nancy Gray Ogle

Kids Can Press acknowledges the financial support of the Government of Ontario, through the Ontario Media Development Corporation's Ontario Book Initiative; the Ontario Arts Council; the Canada Council for the Arts; and the Government of Canada, through the BPIDP, for our publishing activity.

Published in Canada by
Kids Can Press Ltd.
29 Birch Avenue
Toronto, ON M4V 1E2

Published in the U.S. by
Kids Can Press Ltd.
2250 Military Road
Tonawanda, NY 14150

www.kidscanpress.com

Edited by Stacey Roderick
Designed by Marie Bartholomew
Printed and bound in China

The hardcover edition of this book is smyth sewn casebound.
The paperback edition of this book is limp sewn with a drawn-on cover.

CM 06 0 9 8 7 6 5 4 3 2 1
CM PA 06 0 9 8 7 6 5 4 3 2 1

Library and Archives Canada Cataloguing in Publication

Mason, Adrienne
  Skunks / written by Adrienne Mason; illustrated by Nancy Gray Ogle.

(Kids Can Press wildlife series)

Includes index.
ISBN-13: 978-1-55337-733-7 (bound)
ISBN-13: 978-1-55337-734-4 (pbk.)
ISBN-10: 1-55337-733-8 (bound)
ISBN-10: 1-55337-734-6 (pbk.)

1. Skunks—Juvenile literature. I. Ogle, Nancy Gray II. Title. III. Series.

QL737.C248M38 2006   j599.76'8   C2005-903891-8

Kids Can Press is a *Corus*™ Entertainment company

Contents

Skunks

Skunks are small animals that live on land. They have bushy tails and thick, jet-black fur with white markings.

Skunks are most active at night, but sometimes they come out during the day. People rarely see skunks, but they often smell them. Skunks can spray a bad-smelling liquid when they are in danger.

Skunks are mammals. Mammals breathe air using their lungs, give birth to live young and have furry bodies. Mammals are also warm-blooded. This means that their body temperature stays about the same, even when the temperature outside changes.

Striped skunk

The scientific
name for
striped skunks
and hooded
skunks means
"bad odor."

Kinds of skunks

There are four kinds of skunks in North America: spotted, striped, hooded and hog-nosed. The largest skunks, hog-nosed skunks and striped skunks, are about the size of a pet cat. Female skunks are a bit smaller than male skunks.

The hog-nosed skunk has a long, bare snout, like a pig's. This skunk can weigh up to 4.5 kg (10 pounds).

The striped skunk can weigh from 1.5 to 5 kg (3 to 11 pounds).

The spotted skunk is the smallest kind of skunk. A large male weighs about 900 g (32 ounces). That's about as much as four apples.

The hooded skunk has long hair that looks like a hood across its head and neck. This skunk can weigh up to 1.2 kg (2.5 pounds).

Where skunks live

Skunks are found in North America, Central America and South America. Two closely related species are also found in Asia.

Skunks live in many kinds of habitats, from fields to forests. Skunks can live close to people and are often found near farms or even in cities. They live where they can find food and shelter.

The size of a skunk's territory, or the area they live in, depends on the amount of food that is available. If there is a lot of food available, their territory is small. This is because they do not need to travel far to find food.

The striped skunk is the most common skunk in North America.

Where striped skunks live

North America

Striped skunks

SKUNK FACT

A skunk's territory can be as large as 12 city blocks.

Skunk homes

Skunks live in homes called dens. Dens are where skunks rest and hide from enemies. A den can be a burrow in the ground, a hollow tree, a ditch, a rock pile or even a small space under a building.

During the summer, skunk dens are usually above ground. In winter, skunks that live in cold areas find dens below ground. Skunks often use the old burrows of other animals, or they dig their own.

Underground dens often have several entrances, so the skunk can go in one opening and leave by another. Skunks use grasses and leaves to hide the many entrances and to make their dens comfortable.

In cold weather, striped skunks sometimes share their dens with other skunks.

Striped skunk

Skunk bodies

A skunk's body is built for digging and for keeping enemies away. This is a striped skunk.

Ears and nose

Keen senses of hearing and smell help a skunk find its prey, even if the prey is underground.

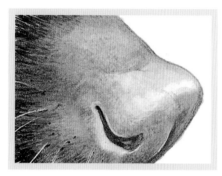

Eyes

A skunk has good close-up sight, but it does not see faraway objects well.

The hog-nosed skunk uses its snout to sniff out and dig for insects. Its nose is protected by a thick pad of skin.

Teeth

Small, sharp teeth are used for grabbing and crunching food.

Claws

Long, curved claws dig for insects and other food. They are also used for digging burrows.

Fur

A skunk has two kinds of fur. The outer hair is long and straight. It keeps out water. The fur next to the skunk's skin is short and wavy. It traps air next to the skunk's skin to help keep it warm.

Tail

The long, bushy tail is raised when warning enemies to stay away.

Musk glands

Musk, or strong-smelling oil, is stored under the skunk's tail in two pouches called glands. The ends of the glands look like the tips of tiny hoses. A skunk sprays the musk when it is in danger.

Paws

Thick skin on the paws protects them from sharp rocks and harmful insects, such as wasps.

How skunks protect themselves

Skunk enemies, or predators, include bobcats, dogs, foxes, coyotes, badgers and birds of prey, such as owls and eagles. Skunks spray musk to defend themselves. But before they spray, they try to frighten their predators away.

First, a skunk will stomp its feet, arch its back and scratch the ground with its claws. If this doesn't scare the other animal, a skunk will hiss, clack its teeth and raise its tail like a warning flag.

When a skunk is ready to spray, it curves its body into a U-shape so both its rear end and head face the predator. Skunks try to aim for their enemy's face and can spray a distance of about 4.5 m (15 feet). They can shoot the oil in a fine mist or in a straight stream. Besides smelling awful, musk stings the eyes of enemies.

A skunk's black-and-white fur is a warning to predators. They know if they get too close, they might get sprayed.

Striped skunk

As a final warning before it sprays musk, a spotted skunk will stand on its front paws.

How skunks move

Skunks usually move slowly. They waddle along on their short legs. Skunks can run short distances, though. They sometimes run to get away from predators or to catch fast-moving prey, such as lizards or mice.

Skunks are able to spin around very quickly. In a flash, they can turn to show their raised tail. This position may scare an enemy away.

Spotted skunks are very good climbers and will climb trees in search of food.

Skunks usually avoid the water but can swim if they have to.

Hooded skunk

17

Skunk food

Skunks are omnivores. This means that they eat both plants and animals.

Skunks eat fruit, vegetables, grass and even cactuses. Their diet also includes mice, lizards and birds, as well as many types of insects, such as grasshoppers, crickets, ants and earwigs. Some skunks even catch fish. Skunks also feed on dead animals, which are called carrion.

Skunk diets change throughout the year depending on what is available. In the spring, they eat mice and other small mammals, birds and bird eggs. In the late summer and fall, they feed heavily on insects, plants and fruit. In the winter, skunks may eat very little.

Western spotted skunk

SKUNK FACT

Skunks will eat snakes — even poisonous rattlesnakes!

19

How skunks gather food

Skunks usually look for food at night. They mainly use their keen senses of smell and hearing to find food.

Skunks sometimes track, or follow, prey. They will pounce on fast-moving animals, such as mice or rabbits.

Some skunks eat bees and wasps. They kill these stinging insects first by rolling them between their thick-skinned paws. Skunks also roll caterpillars between their paws before eating them to remove any sharp spines.

Skunks are expert insect hunters. They use their long front claws to dig in soil or logs to find insects. Sometimes they even peel back chunks of grass to get at the insects underneath.

Some skunks
toss eggs back
through their
legs to crack
the shells and
eat them.

White-backed
hog-nosed skunk

21

Skunks and their young

Baby skunks are usually born in the spring. Mothers give birth to one to twelve babies in a litter. They sometimes have two litters in one year. Skunk fathers don't help to raise the babies.

Baby skunks are called kits. Kits are born with their eyes closed and without a lot of fur.

Newborn kits drink their mother's milk. They stay close to their mother and snuggle with her and with their brothers and sisters to keep warm and safe. If the mother has to move the kits, she bites onto the loose skin on the back of their necks. Being picked up this way doesn't hurt them.

Kits have musk when they are as young as three days old.

Even though newborn kits have very little fur, a black-and-white pattern shows on their pink skin.

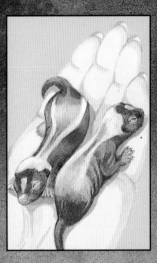

Newborn kits are so small you could hold two in the palm of your hand.

23

How skunks grow and learn

Baby skunks grow quickly. At one week old, their weight is double what it was at birth. By the time the kits are one month old, they have grown fur and opened their eyes. When they are about six weeks old, the kits play in the burrow and eat food other than their mother's milk.

Mother skunks teach their young how to hunt and dig for food. To learn, the young skunks follow their mother and copy everything she does.

Skunks are almost full grown by the time they are three months old. By then, they can gather their own food and defend themselves by spraying musk.

In the fall, most young skunks set out on their own.

Most wild skunks live for two to three years.

Young skunks, like these spotted skunks, follow their mother in a line, one after the other.

Skunks and people

Skunks often live close to where people live. This is because skunks find shelter and food near cities and farms. Living near people and cities can be dangerous for skunks, though. Since skunks are active at night and slow moving, many are accidentally killed on roads and highways.

Some people dislike skunks because they can leave a bad smell in the air and because they sometimes eat birds, bird eggs, fruits and vegetables. But skunks also help people by eating a lot of animals that can be pests, such as insects, rats and mice.

People sometimes keep skunks as pets. These skunks have had their musk glands removed. Skunks do not make good pets, and in many places it is illegal to keep them.

In some places, biologists and educators are trying to teach people about the importance of protecting wild skunks in nature.

Striped skunks

Skunks of the world

The skunk family includes stink badgers as well as skunks. Here are some of the skunks and stink badgers that live around the world.

North America

White-backed hog-nosed skunk

Pygmy spotted skunk

Western spotted skunk

Striped skunk

Hooded skunk

Eastern spotted skunk

Central and South America

Striped hog-nosed skunk

Southern spotted skunk

Patagonian hog-nosed skunk

South American hog-nosed skunk

Asia

Philippine stink badger

Sunda stink badger

Skunk signs

Tracks

Skunk tracks show where skunks have dug their five long claws into the soil. The two striped-skunk footprints shown here are actual size.

Musk scent

A strong smell of musk in the air is a clue that skunks were nearby.

Scat

Scat is the name for animal droppings or body waste. Some skunk scat has a strong, musky odor.

Fur

When skunks squeeze through small openings, they sometimes leave a few long black or white hairs behind.

Diggings

Cone-shaped holes in a lawn or a field are a sign that skunks have been digging for food.

Words to know

burrow: a hole in the ground where skunks can live

carrion: a dead animal

den: a shelter for skunks

habitat: a place where an animal naturally lives and grows

kit: a baby skunk

litter: a group of kits born to a mother skunk

musk: a smelly oil that skunks spray from musk glands

omnivore: an animal that eats other animals and plants

predator: an animal that hunts other animals

prey: an animal that is hunted for food

Index